LEONARDO DA VINCI'S
LIFE OF INVENTION

To all my friends and family for their continued love and support – Jake Williams

First published in Great Britain in 2022 by Pavilion Children's Books
This edition published in Great Britain in 2022 by Red Shed, part of Farshore
An imprint of HarperCollins*Publishers*
1 London Bridge Street, London SE1 9GF
www.farshore.co.uk

HarperCollins*Publishers*
Macken House, 39/40 Mayor Street Upper,
Dublin 1, D01 C9W8

ISBN: 978 1 8436 5498 8
Printed at Oriental Press, Dubai
002

A CIP catalogue record for this book is available from the British Library.

Stay safe online. Any website addresses listed in this book are correct at the time of going to print. However, Farshore is not responsible for content hosted by third parties. Please be aware that online content can be subject to change and websites can contain content that is unsuitable for children. We advise that all children are supervised when using the internet.

Farshore takes its responsibility to the planet and its inhabitants very seriously.
We aim to use papers from well-managed forests run by responsible suppliers.

LEONARDO DA VINCI'S LIFE OF INVENTION

JAKE WILLIAMS

RED SHED

Contents

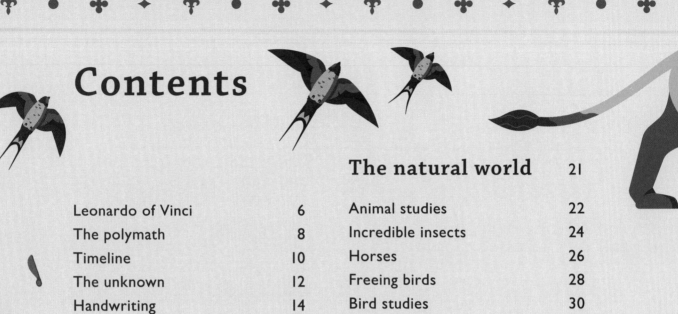

Leonardo of Vinci

Leonardo da Vinci was born on 15 April 1452 to a notary called Piero da Vinci and a young woman called Caterina di Meo Lippi. Leonardo's parents were not married, and it meant that he could not inherit his father's business. Instead, Leonardo focused on his passions of learning, inventing and painting.

We know him as Leonardo da Vinci, but that isn't actually his real name. Unlike most people today, Leonardo didn't have an official surname and Leonardo da Vinci simply means Leonardo of Vinci — Vinci being the small town in Tuscany, Italy, where he was born.

Even from a young age, it was clear that Leonardo was incredibly talented. He had an unquenchable thirst for knowledge matched with an amazing imagination and exceptional artistic skill. Although little is known about his early life, it was clear that Leonardo's abilities would take him far beyond the small rural town he grew up in.

Success or failure?

Da Vinci often thought of himself as a failure because much of his work was unfinished, but it's clear to us now that he was an incredible talent — so even if you can't always finish something, it doesn't mean you've failed! As we journey through the life and work of Leonardo da Vinci, we will discover his many successes — from incredible and forward-thinking inventions to stunning paintings — as well as a few of his less successful projects.

The polymath

Leonardo da Vinci was a true polymath. A polymath is someone whose knowledge spans many different areas and subjects. As you'll discover throughout this book, Leonardo's skills and talents went well beyond painting. From art to biology, mathematics to music, his talents knew no bounds!

Da Vinci's creativity took on many forms throughout his life, the most famous of which was his astonishing talent with a paintbrush and canvas. However, he was also a keen musician who could play a range of instruments, and was rumoured to be a fantastic singer too.

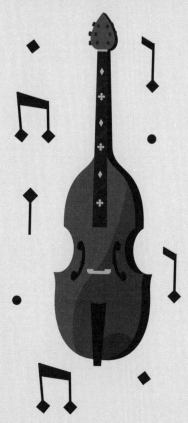

This artistic creativity, combined with his extensive mathematical ability, meant that Leonardo was also able to turn his hand to architecture. Over the course of his lifetime, he drew and designed many structures including bridges, fortresses and walkways.

Much of his work showed his love of the natural world. He could often be found sketching alley cats, horses, plants and flowers in his journals.

Leonardo's various interests often came together. Drawing inspiration from nature helped him to come up with many of his inventions, and his painting and drawing ability helped when studying and documenting the human body. Da Vinci's work is evidence of how different interests and skills can work together to create unique and unexpected outcomes.

Leonardo da Vinci lived and worked over 500 years ago during the Renaissance period. Now the medieval period was over (a time when knights in gleaming suits of armour were a common sight) there were lots of exciting and important events in history about to take place.

Leonardo da Vinci
1452–1519
Leonardo lived during the Renaissance period (approximately 1400–1600)

The Medieval Period
476–1400s
This began in 476 CE with the Fall of Rome

The Age of Exploration
1400–1600s
A period of overseas exploration and colonisation by European countries

William Shakespeare
1564–1616

The famous English playwright wrote
Romeo and Juliet in around 1595

The Age of
Enlightenment
1600–1800

This period saw greater interest in
sciences like astronomy from a more
literate and educated public

The unknown

While out for a gentle walk one day, a young Leonardo da Vinci decided to venture off the beaten path. After journeying for some time, he stumbled across the intimidating entrance to a large and dark cave. Immediately, Leonardo was intrigued by what he saw but also frozen in fear: he wasn't scared by the appearance of a monster or a wild animal, but by the unknown that might lurk in the impenetrable darkness in front of him. Try as he might to see what was inside, there was no way of knowing without venturing further in.

After much deliberation, Leonardo's curiosity about what lay within the cave won out. He took a deep breath, calmed his nerves and headed inside. Once through the mouth of the cave, da Vinci was rewarded with the beautiful sight of ancient fossils lining the walls. The experience had a big impact on Leonardo, reminding him that working through fear can give you the opportunity to experience something amazing!

Some historians think that Leonardo's account of the fossils in the cave might be one of the first descriptions of a fossilised whale skeleton.

Handwriting

Leonardo took his handwriting skills one step further than most people. His usual writing hand was his left, but after a lot of practice and scribbled sheets of paper, he also taught himself to write with his right hand. The ability to use both your right and left hands equally well is called being ambidextrous.

This ability wasn't just limited to writing for da Vinci, and he could also draw with both hands. Try writing your name with your normal writing hand, then swap it to try with your opposite hand and see how difficult it is!

Can you draw with your opposite hand too?

Just in case you thought he couldn't be any more of a genius, Leonardo also sometimes wrote from right to left and formed the words backwards. The exact reason that he did this remains unclear, but it could have been a way to keep his hands clean — writing in this direction with his left hand would avoid smudging the words as he wrote.

If you can read this writing — well done! Lots of Leonardo's writing can only be read when held up to a mirror.

One of Leonardo's most famous works, the Vitruvian Man, features mirror writing (see page 70).

The Renaissance

Leonardo da Vinci lived during a period of history called the Renaissance. This began over 600 years ago in the 15th century, and it lasted for around 200 years. The Renaissance started in Florence, Italy, just a short trip from Leonardo's hometown of Vinci, before spreading across Europe. Leonardo would spend many years of his life in Florence and go on to contribute greatly to the Renaissance era.

The Renaissance is a French word meaning 'rebirth', and it was a time when Classical wisdom and learning in subjects such as science, art, music and culture were very important. Changes in society meant that people became more educated, and life started to become more like the way we live it today. This time period also popularised the belief that humankind's achievements should be celebrated.

The main currency at the time was the florin, a gold coin from Florence. Since many rich merchants and banks were based in the city, the florin was used for trade across Europe.

Renaissance Italy was split up into
several different regions known
as city-states. These worked a
little like separate countries, with
their own different leaders and
wealth. City-states often had a
speciality that set them apart from
neighbouring regions. Florence
was known for its art and textile
production, whereas Venice had
a thriving navy.

Vinci to Florence

Florence

After showing amazing artistic talent from a young age, Leonardo da Vinci was sent to be an apprentice to the famous painter and sculptor Andrea del Verrocchio. This meant packing his bags and setting off from his hometown of Vinci for the thriving city life of Florence. It's not known for sure how old Leonardo was, but he might have been just 15 when he left home.

Under del Verrocchio's tuition, Leonardo learned the basics of Renaissance painting. First he mastered how to prepare paints and a canvas, before moving on to drawing techniques, proportions and figures. During this time it was common for single paintings to be undertaken by a group of artists, not just one individual. This would have given da Vinci the opportunity to practise painting the smaller elements of an artwork before taking on his own complete masterpiece.

✤ ❖ The natural ❖ ✤
world

Animal studies

We know that animals and nature formed a big part of Leonardo's artistic and scientific interests. He was mesmerised by their abilities, qualities and interactions with one another. From the notes he wrote over the years, he is thought to have been a keen vegetarian and did not like the idea of eating meat. Growing up in a small village around lots of animals could have been what sparked his early passion for creatures.

In Leonardo's work, we can see drawings of all kinds of animals from crabs and lions, to horses and insects. In one of his notebooks, he even drew 26 studies of cats and lions on a single page!

Leonardo would sketch and study each animal as much as possible before putting them in his finished artworks. This dedication to studying and illustrating all creatures in such intricate detail is evidence of his true love for the natural world. His passion for learning about animals went beyond simply drawing them and Leonardo also often pondered their thoughts and emotions.

Incredible insects

Leonardo da Vinci's curiosity about the natural world was not limited to large animals. Insects were just as fascinating to him, and anything that flew, walked or scuttled could give him an idea for his next invention.

Flight

Leonardo had a constant interest in flight and flying machines. Birds and bats were his primary source of inspiration, but he would also study the flight patterns and wing movements of insects. By drawing the different positions and patterns the wings formed to help the insect fly, da Vinci hoped to discover the secret to human flight!

The longhorn beetle

It wasn't just flying insects that interested
Leonardo, he also drew a whole range of
other bugs such as this longhorn beetle.
The antennae of these beetles can grow
to well over their own body length in size!

Amazing ants

Even creatures such as the common
ant can be seen sketched throughout
Leonardo's journals. Perhaps it was their
amazing ability to work as a team that
interested him — or maybe it was how
ants can carry leaves many times the
weight of their own body!

Singing cicada

Another insect that can be found
in da Vinci's drawings is the cicada.
These large insects make loud clicking
or humming sounds, with each species
having a unique call similar to how
humans have different accents.

Horses

One species that Leonardo found particularly interesting was the horse. During the Renaissance, horses were a key part of daily life. They were used for transport, farming and merchant trading, as well as war. Living in the busy city of Florence, da Vinci was often around these incredible animals.

The way horses moved was something Leonardo da Vinci could often be seen sketching. From a lightning-fast gallop to a gentle trot, Leonardo studied it all. Horses can run at nearly 50 kilometres per hour, so he would have certainly needed to be quick with his chalk and paper to capture that!

*Horses can stand and walk
within hours of being born!*

Da Vinci was asked by the Duke of Milan to create a giant horse statue, so big that it would have needed 70 tonnes of bronze to make — that's the weight of roughly 10 African elephants! Unfortunately, this statue became one of Leonardo's several unfinished works, as the bronze he needed was used for the production of military cannons instead.

Studying horse anatomy helped da Vinci to understand how humans and animals worked on the inside and some of the similarities between them. For example, horses' hooves are made out of keratin, which is the same material as your fingernails and toenails.

Freeing birds

In 15th-century Italy, birds were often sold at markets as food or to be kept as pets. Being passionate about nature, Leonardo did not like this one bit. He believed it was a cruel practice and longed for those birds to be free to fly and explore the open landscape.

So da Vinci did something which seemed very strange to everyone at the time. He would make his way through bustling marketplaces in search of poor caged birds and when he spotted them in their cramped metal cages, instead of buying them to take home he simply opened the cage doors. Leonardo wanted to release the animals so they were free to soar through the skies once more.

Birds have hollow bones, meaning their skeletons are very light. This makes flying much easier!

Bird studies

Leonardo studied birds and their flight in great depth. He spent lots of time looking at the structure of their wings to learn how they moved and helped the bird fly. Da Vinci also noticed how a bird's weight affects its flight, an important factor when considering how to lift a human off the ground — we weigh a lot more than most birds!

Birds moult, which means their old or damaged feathers fall out to make way for a fresh new set.

A bird's wing is made up of a series of small bones creating the main structure, where a sequence of keratin feathers are attached. You might remember keratin from da Vinci's study of horses — it's the same material that makes up horses' hooves and human fingernails.

Wings are very important in flight. Birds need a stream of moving air to take off — they can create this stream by moving their wings and using their bodies to jump into the air, or they can use wind to help them. Wings are specially shaped so that the moving stream of air moves more quickly over the top of the wing than beneath it. This creates a lift force, keeping the bird airborne.

All his research on birds greatly influenced Leonardo's later inventions where he explored the possibilities of human flight in his many ideas for flying machines.

Blackberries

Spray of oak leaves
and acorns

Plant studies

Da Vinci's love for nature didn't stop at the animal kingdom, but included the entire natural world. His sketches of all sorts of interesting plants not only helped to develop his artistic talents, but also fed into his scientific knowledge and understanding of the natural world.

Lilies

Star of Bethlehem flowers

Human anatomy

Leonardo studied human anatomy to create some of the most important, masterful and in-depth drawings of human biology from the time. He went into great detail, showing various parts of the body from a range of different angles. These detailed breakdowns of anatomy helped him explore exactly how the human body functioned, not only contributing to medicine of the time but also making discoveries that are still relevant today.

By understanding what bones or muscles looked like underneath the skin, da Vinci had a serious advantage when recreating the human form in art. Some artists of the time may have altered what the body looked like when painting people, but da Vinci was focused on accuracy and correct proportions in his work.

Da Vinci's medical studies often focused on joints and bones, and how our interconnected skeleton allows us to stand, walk and move. Today we know that there are around 206 bones in the body with 33 vertebrae in the spine and around 26 bones just in the foot. With all those bones, da Vinci certainly had a lot of work documenting an entire human skeleton.

Even more gruesomely, Leonardo also studied the inner workings of human organs. He was likely the first person in history to discover the four chambers of a human heart! These detailed studies of the human body not only aided medical science, but also helped da Vinci to create more accurate human figures in his artwork.

Comparing humans and animals

Da Vinci was constantly observing the world around him, searching for patterns and similarities that would help his understanding of nature and human beings.

Leonardo would study the muscle and bone structure of both humans and animals to compare how their different anatomies helped each creature move. This is called comparative anatomy, and for da Vinci included looking at the similarities between a human's leg and a dog's leg.

There are lots of surprising anatomical comparisons to make between humans and animals. For example, giraffes have seven neck verterbrae — the same number as humans, although each one is quite a lot larger to get that long neck!

You might not think that a human and an onion have much in common, and for the most part you'd be right. But Leonardo likened the individual layers that make up the inside of an onion to the layers of a human scalp, including the skull, skin and hair.

Leonardo's interest in animals went beyond just anatomy. He was also fascinated by the different moods and emotions of animals such as cats and dogs.

If you have pets, can you tell when they're feeling happy or sad? What do they do to show they are sleepy or excited?

Dragons

Perhaps some of the most surprising things to see in da Vinci's journals are his drawings of mythical dragons. Certainly not something you'd expect to see flying over the cobbled streets of Florence, or anywhere for that matter! However these strange made-up creatures appear several times throughout his sketchbooks and with the internet still well over 450 years away from being invented, Leonardo had to use his seemingly endless imagination to come up with these beasts.

It seems like sketching mythical creatures was something of a fun hobby for da Vinci, as dragons weren't the only strange beasts he drew. If you search through the depths of his journals you'll come across all manner of creatures, from basilisks to horses with fish-like tails. This likely gave Leonardo a well-earned change from his accurate artworks of the natural world as he drew from his imagination instead.

Milan

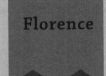
Florence

Florence to Milan

In 1482 at the age of 30, da Vinci left life as a successful painter in Florence and headed to work for the regent of Milan, Ludovico Sforza. Ludovico governed Milan while the real Duke, his nephew Gian Galeazzo, was too young to rule.

Although painting remained a big part of da Vinci's daily life, it seems that one of the main reasons for Leonardo's move to Milan was to develop his work in architecture, engineering and inventing. Leonardo wrote to Ludovico Sforza describing his skill as a military engineer and it was in Milan that he came up with many of his inventions for the battlefield.

Inventions

Armoured car

One of da Vinci's more outlandish inventions was the armoured car, designed to catch the attention of the regent and Duke of Milan. Unlike many carts at the time, this invention could move not only forwards and backwards but also side to side. It had sloped edges to protect itself from enemies and attackers. As with many of his inventions, Leonardo likely drew inspiration for this design from the animal kingdom: the hard exterior of the car is similar to the shell of a tortoise, turtle or even a snail!

One problem with this design was that the wooden cranks, used to move the wheels, were actually set up incorrectly. According to da Vinci's plans, the cranks were the wrong way round, making it very difficult for the car to move. The reason for this may never be known, but one possibility could have been to deter potential copy-cats and keep his designs secret!

To get the armoured car moving, several men would have to get inside and turn the heavy wooden cranks that, through a system of cogs, would get the wheels spinning. Like many of Leonardo da Vinci's military inventions, the armoured car was designed more for intimidation than actual function. Moving towards the enemy during battle, the cart's massive size and many cannons would certainly give anyone a fright and hopefully put the enemy at a disadvantage. From its shape, wheels and hard exterior, it is clear to see the similarities between tanks around today and da Vinci's curious invention.

Automated cart

Although a self-driving cart may sound like something from science fiction, it was actually another one of Leonardo's futuristic inventions. Long before the modern car had been thought of, he came up with the idea of a self-propelled, automatically steered cart that could be programmed before it set off.

The machine worked in a similar way to a wind-up toy. It moved by using a complicated series of cogs, wheels and gears attached to two symmetrical springs that stored the energy needed to propel the cart forwards. Da Vinci's design even featured a system that would allow the user to re-programme the steering for the cart. However there was one problem with this design: the vehicle could only turn right, so despite being ahead of its time in lots of ways, it would have been stuck going around in circles! The ideas and technology of this design can be seen all around us today, from modern cars that can steer themselves to the clockwork components found inside wristwatches.

Unlike today's cars, Leonardo's cart wasn't used for transport but instead for theatre performances and festivals. It was designed to inspire wonder and amazement in the audience who had likely never seen a machine move on its own before — similar to you suddenly seeing your desk roll across the room on its own!

The parachute and more

Portable bridge

One of Leonardo's designs that likely never left his sketchbook was his portable bridge. This was a truly innovative design as it did not require any equipment or tools to set up and use. The structure of the bridge was designed to be strong and sturdy without any supports beneath. Da Vinci's idea behind this was that the bridge could be easily carried and set up wherever needed — clever!

Anemometer — a wind speed measuring device

Da Vinci created an adaptation of an anemometer which allowed him to determine the speed and direction of the wind. The wind would blow the hanging piece of wood up the scale to give an indication of speed, and the arrow sat on top of the device showed the direction of the wind.

The parachute

It's possible that da Vinci was one of the first people to invent and design a parachute. The parachute was made by stretching a piece of fabric over a structure of wooden poles in the shape of a pyramid. It's amazing to think that da Vinci came up with this invention so long ago, and it remains largely unchanged to this day!

Giant crossbow

Instead of arrows, like a normal crossbow, Leonardo designed this fearsome weapon to fire large objects, rocks, even noisy gunpowder artillery! To fire this crossbow, someone would need to heave a heavy wooden crank to draw the bow back into its firing position. Next, the object being fired would be placed in position and then the bow would be released by hitting out a holding pin with a hammer. Much like his armoured car, it was more about scaring the opposition than being an effective weapon. Horses could easily be scared by the enormous size and sound — forget an actual cannonball, even just the mighty crack of the bow would be enough to give you a sudden fright!

The idea of firing flaming cannonballs has fascinated many throughout history and you can imagine how terrifying they would be to see hurtling through the sky. It wouldn't be possible to fire them from a wooden crossbow, however.

The crossbow would have been constructed out of thin wood to give it extra flexibility and fire its projectiles even further.

The crossbow featured six giant wooden wheels to allow it to move around, particularly useful if you needed to reposition it during the heat of battle. Many people would be needed to move the giant crossbow though, as this huge mechanical contraption would have weighed an unimaginable amount and measured over 20 metres across.

The average human is around 1.7 metres (5 feet 6 inches) tall, meaning 11 people could lie head to toe and still not be the same width as this machine!

Studying flight

On a warm Italian summer's evening, you can picture da Vinci watching the flittering wings of a sparrow, the swish and glide of a swallow, or the flutter of a bee. He longed to accomplish the difficult task of human flight, and this lifelong goal inspired an array of madcap mechanical contraptions that would all attempt to lift a human being up, up and away into the sky. The next time you see a bird flying through the sky, maybe you'll be inspired to create your own curious invention.

The mechanical bat

Leonardo's fascination with flight was something that continued throughout his life. Many of da Vinci's notebooks and journals were filled with strange flying machines and aerial contraptions. One of these fascinating machines was his mechanical bat.

Leonardo studied the wing structure, flight and movement of small bats. You can see the wooden structure of the mechanical bat's wings are actually very similar to those of the real animal. So you could say that da Vinci invented the original Batmobile!

Da Vinci never completed this invention, but with today's knowledge we now recognise that although it may have been able to glide, it was very unlikely this contraption would ever lift off the ground without some kind of engine. The creative thinking behind this invention was truly astounding though and has fascinated inventors for centuries!

Da Vinci's design featured a tail for extra stability while the vehicle was in flight.

In order to lift a human up into the air, Leonardo calculated the wingspan of this machine would have to be huge — over 20 metres (around 66 feet)!

Stirrups were connected to the wings. The pilot could push into these to make the wings flap, much like a real bat or bird.

Helicopter

In his continuing quest for flight, da Vinci sketched an invention he named the aerial screw. This curious contraption looked and worked in many ways similar to the modern day helicopter. However, Leonardo da Vinci came up with this over 400 years before the modern helicopter was ever built — talk about thinking ahead of your time!

As he so often did, it's likely da Vinci got his inspiration for this device from nature. This time, rather than being inspired by a darting dragonfly or the swish of a bird's wing, he looked up instead to see sycamore seeds falling and gently spiralling downwards. He wondered — if the seeds spun in one direction while falling, perhaps when they were spun in the opposite direction, they could rise. Although this machine did not successfully fly, da Vinci's idea lives on in the helicopter today.

Robot knight

Meeting this seemingly empty suit of Renaissance armour could certainly give you a fright: it was capable of moving completely on its own! From the outside, it may look like a normal suit of armour, but on the inside lies what many believe to be the world's first ever robot.

Modern robots use a series of high-tech electronics, wires, circuits and motors. However, da Vinci made several robots using resources available to him at the time such as wood, rope and metal. Underneath the fearsome outer armour of this robot knight was a metal skeleton. Wooden discs were then mounted onto this and attached to one another with rope or twine. Much like da Vinci's self-propelled cart, the robot knight used springs to store the energy needed to move. Once these springs were released, they would pull on the ropes connected to the wooden discs, and in turn would make the knight move. Simple but effective! Although the knight might not have been able to do the robot dance move, it did have many other actions it could perform on its own. The armour could raise or lower its visor and helmet, stand up and sit down. One of da Vinci's robots could even tap a beat on a drum!

Diving suit

So far, Leonardo da Vinci's inventions have taken us up, up and away with his flying machines, turned us in circles with his self-propelled cart, and given us a fright with his robot knight — but now it's time to venture somewhere a little wetter, under the sea!

Da Vinci's next outlandish invention was an underwater diving suit. It was designed to allow the diver to breathe underwater by connecting long tubes to a bell-shaped device that would float on the water's surface. The bell would be full of air for the diver to breathe. Sandbags attached to the suit's belt helped the diver to sink all the way down to the very depths of the seabed. Then they would be able to walk along the seafloor, much like an astronaut on the moon.

The original idea behind this suit was to allow soldiers to creep along the ocean bed, up to enemy ships. The divers could then sabotage these ships from underneath, without ever coming up for air. Very sneaky!

Leonardo wanted the wearer to be able to stay underwater for as long as possible. However, this came with a crucial problem: what happened when the diver needed a wee? Well, da Vinci thought of this and even included a little bottle for the diver to go to the bathroom in!

No wonder Leonardo's mind was on maritime matters — at the time he designed the diving suit he was living amongst the canals of Venice, the floating city!

Planetshine

Have you ever looked up into a clear night's sky when the moon is just a slither and noticed a glow outlining the shape of the rest of the moon? This soft shine was something da Vinci puzzled over for many years. The effect can be hard to see nowadays due to light pollution from street lamps, cars and buildings, but it would have been easy to see during the Renaissance when da Vinci was alive.

Up until this point, many people had marvelled at this strange phenomenon of a glowing moon, but nobody could explain why it happened. During the lunar cycle, the moon and Earth move through different positions around the sun. At different points in the moon's cycle around Earth, the amount of the sun's light that we can see shining onto the surface of the moon from our position on Earth changes. This is why sometimes you see a full moon, sometimes a half moon and sometimes a crescent moon.

But why would you see a glowing outline shining back from the area of the moon that should be in shadow? Da Vinci theorised that some of the sunlight hitting the Earth might be reflected onto the moon, then reflected again from the moon back to Earth. All that bouncing around makes the light much dimmer, which is why we only see a very faint glowing outline of the moon's surface. We now know da Vinci was correct in his theory, and today the effect is known as planetshine.

It is said that da Vinci was able to play many stringed instruments, including a large, violin-like instrument called the lira da braccio. He was said to have a fine singing voice too — it seems there was very little this man couldn't do!

Musical talents

Da Vinci contributed to the development of many musical instruments over the years, and even designed a brand new instrument known as the viola organista. This was a strange object, much like a combination of a violin and a piano. The viola organista featured an automated bow that played taut violin-like strings you selected with keys, similar to a piano.

Leonardo enjoyed the science behind music just as much as he enjoyed actually playing and composing music. His journals featured many entries on the science of sound (acoustics). One of his acoustic experiments was listening through a long tube in water — he realised he was able to hear ships far away, and so he's often credited as one of the first people to realise that sound travels in waves!

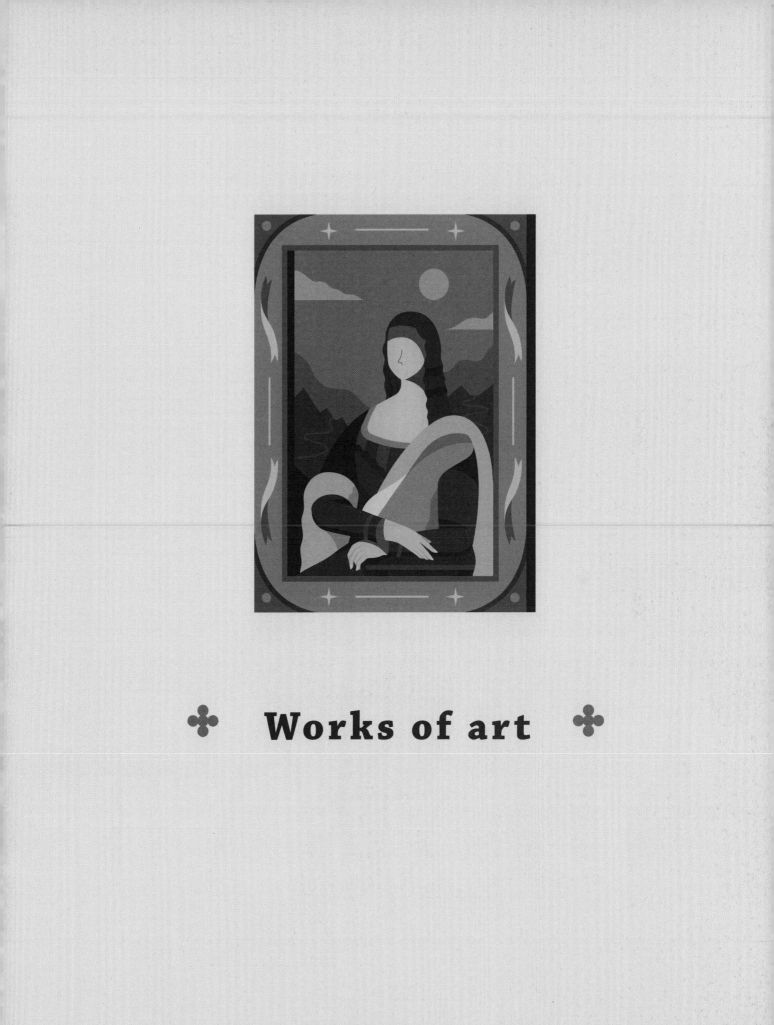

✤ **Works of art** ✤

Da Vinci's workshop

Welcome to da Vinci's wonderful workshop!
Full of Renaissance tools, paints, palettes and
wooden canvases. His artistic abilities are
perhaps what da Vinci is most famous for, and
he has gone down in history as one of the most
accomplished and talented painters of all time.

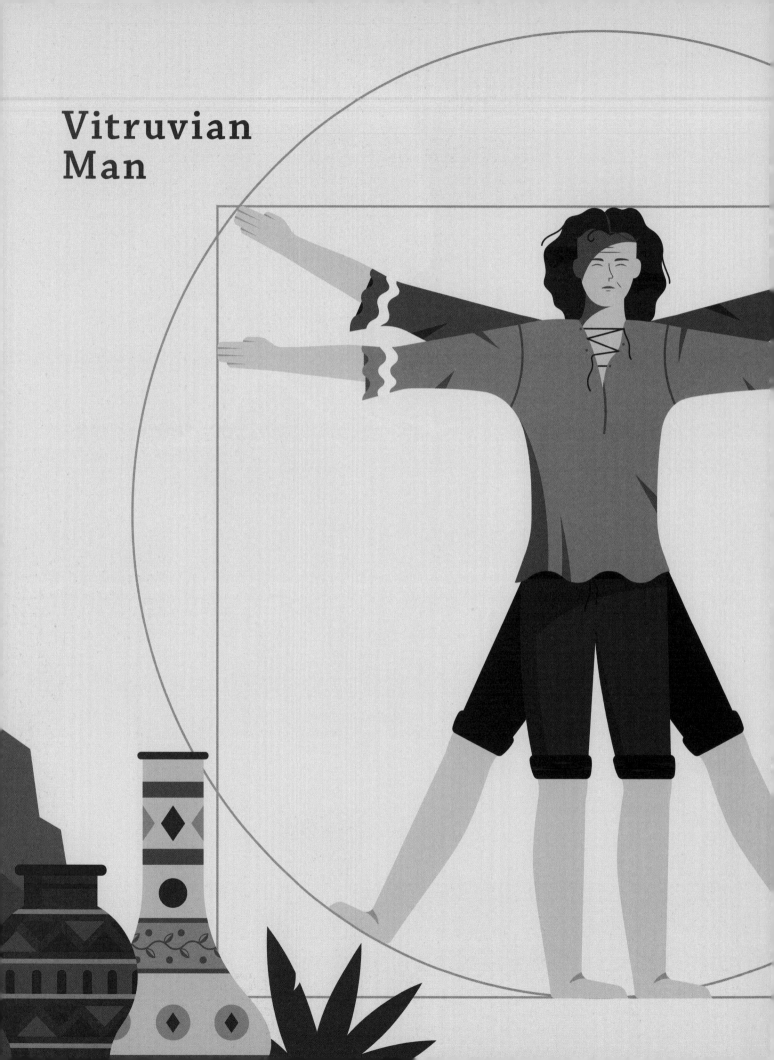

Vitruvian Man

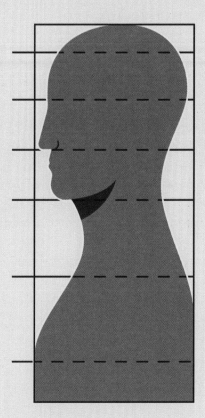

Da Vinci spent much of his life drawing, sketching and studying human beings. In order to more accurately recreate the human form in his art, he would measure the distance between points on the human body — for example the distance between the eyes and the nose. This scientific approach helped da Vinci to set himself apart from other artists of the time by drawing incredibly realistic and accurate human figures.

The most famous of these drawings is the Vitruvian Man. Da Vinci's drawing features a character who fits perfectly inside both square and circle guidelines. Leonardo saw these as the perfect proportions for the human body. At first glance it may only appear to be two poses but there are actually 16 different combinations of positions. Take a closer look and see if you can identify them all!

The Mona Lisa

The Mona Lisa is probably the most famous painting in the world today. This iconic painting has a long and fascinating history full of love, theft and mystery. We don't know the exact date he started painting it, but it was likely around 1503 when he still lived in Florence. Leonardo spent many long years toiling away with his extensive range of oil paints to perfect this masterpiece. So many years, in fact, that the painting remained in his workshop until his death in 1519. Looking at the Mona Lisa, you may think it was painted on canvas. However, like most of da Vinci's works, it is actually painted on a white sheet of wood called poplar.

One of the many mysteries surrounding the painting is the identity of the subject. This would be much easier to figure out if there was someone famous called Mona Lisa in history, but unfortunately this isn't the case. The painting is thought to be a portrait of Renaissance noblewoman Lisa Gherardini, and likely was commissioned as a gift from her husband Francesco del Giocondo.

Unlike many paintings of the time, the landscape in the background is not based on a real location — instead it is completely made up. Most historical artists would draw something this vast and detailed from life to help them achieve a realistic scene. However with his immense creativity, da Vinci was able to create a completely fictional landscape.

Is the Mona Lisa smiling?

Although it may not be very obvious, she actually is. Most paintings at this time wouldn't have featured their models smiling — perhaps the other artists thought they would be taken more seriously if all their portraits had very serious expressions. But da Vinci intentionally gave the Mona Lisa a slight smile as a way of making her seem merry and lively.

Today the Mona Lisa hangs in a heavily guarded section of the Louvre Museum in Paris, France — but more on that to come . . .

The stolen Mona Lisa

Although today the Mona Lisa might be the most famous painting in the world, this wasn't always the case. So what happened to help this work of art go from just another Renaissance portrait to a world-renowned icon? You might be shocked to find out that it was actually stolen!

The year was 1911, and the Mona Lisa was just another beautiful painting among many beautiful paintings hanging in the Louvre. But one morning French artist Louis Béroud noticed something strange while he walked along the halls of the gallery . . . the Mona Lisa was missing! The Louvre quickly closed and an investigation was hastily launched by the French police to solve the mystery of the missing Mona Lisa.

Initially, world-famous artist Pablo Picasso was one of the main suspects for the theft. This celebrity suspect drew even more attention and public interest surrounding the disappearance of da Vinci's final masterpiece. Later, Picasso was released and all suspicions that he might be the thief were proved false, but this still left the real culprit yet to be found.

After much investigation, the real thief turned out to be a man called Vincenzo Peruggia who was an employee at the Louvre. During the early 1900s there certainly wouldn't have been any high-tech cameras, alarms or security systems in the gallery. This meant it was actually relatively easy for Peruggia to steal the Mona Lisa. He simply hid in a store cupboard until the gallery had closed before grabbing the painting, slipping it under his coat and walking out.

Peruggia felt the painting should have been returned to da Vinci's home country of Italy — where Vincenzo Peruggia was born and raised — which it may have done if it hadn't been for one crafty art dealer. When Peruggia tried to sell the painting to him, the art dealer quickly realised this was the real Mona Lisa and informed the authorities. The painting was swiftly returned to the Louvre, where it remains to this day.

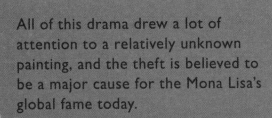

All of this drama drew a lot of attention to a relatively unknown painting, and the theft is believed to be a major cause for the Mona Lisa's global fame today.

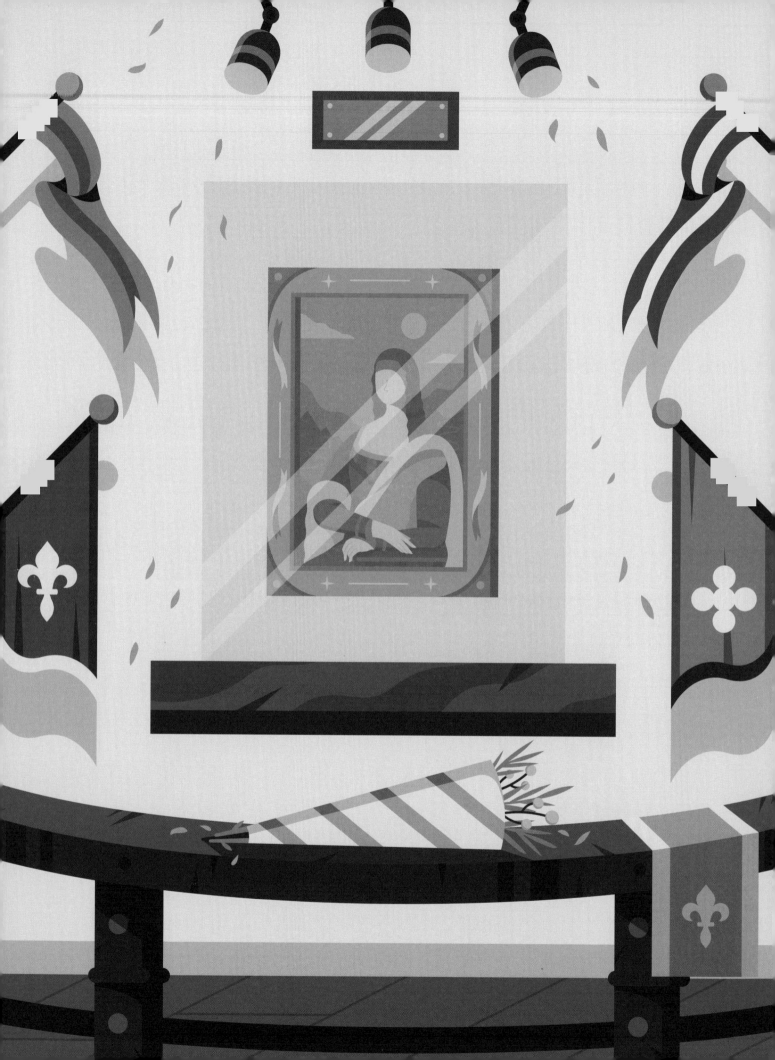

The Mona Lisa in the modern day

It's clear that the Mona Lisa stands today as one of the all-time great works of art. The painting is known all around the world and is frequently referenced in art, music and films. In fact the painting is so loved that it even receives flowers, gifts and letters from admirers.

Da Vinci's masterpiece is essentially priceless, but the Mona Lisa also brings in money. The painting attracts people from all over the world, generating a huge amount of income for the Louvre and for Paris. Over 10 million people visit the museum every year and many go just to gaze upon the mysterious Mona Lisa for themselves.

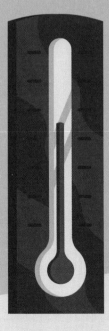

Following its theft in 1911, many high tech security measures have been put into place to make it very difficult to steal or damage the Mona Lisa ever again. Due to its age, this portrait needs very special treatment to ensure the paint and wooden canvas don't break down or deteriorate over time. The Louvre maintains a constant temperature that is close to 20° Celsius with very little moisture in the air.

The Mona Lisa even has a one-of-a-kind lamp that was specially developed to reduce ultraviolet light which can damage the painting.

Portrait of a Musician

Little is known about this mysterious painting, but what we do know is that like many of da Vinci's works, it remains unfinished. Interestingly, it's one of the few portraits that Leonardo painted of a male figure that we know about. One of the mysteries we have been left to ponder is who is in the painting. Was it a famous Renaissance musician that da Vinci liked? Maybe it was a self-portrait of him holding a musical composition? Sadly it's likely that the answer will be forever lost.

Centuries after it was painted, the hand holding sheet music at the bottom of the scene was uncovered during restoration work. This was the major clue to art historians that the portrait was in fact of a musician. What this music might have sounded like is unknown as the painting is in such poor condition that making out individual notes is currently impossible. However this painting is still another fascinating example of how da Vinci's many talents and interests often came together to create stunning outcomes.

A lost Leonardo

Leonardo set out to create a fresco in a Council Hall building while he was living in Florence, but to this day the fabled painting has never officially been discovered. It's often referred to as 'the lost Leonardo'! The only reason we know about this painting at all is through da Vinci's sketches that he made in preparation for the mural.

So where could this lost masterpiece be? Some time later, the walls of that very same Council Hall were painted by an artist named Giorgio Vasari. Many years passed, until one day a cryptic message in Vasari's murals was discovered. Historians and scholars translated the message to read 'Seek and you shall find', leading some to believe that Leonardo's lost painting is still hidden behind that very wall in Florence today!

Attempts have been made to try and look behind the painting to reclaim 'the lost Leonardo'. Modern scientists drilled tiny holes in the wall and have found the same paint pigments that da Vinci used on his famous Mona Lisa. Unfortunately, they cannot keep using this method to uncover more as there is too much risk of damaging Vasari's painting that still remains on the wall, so for now the mystery of 'the lost Leonardo' remains unsolved.

The Warrior

As you look at this regal warrior you can imagine the sounds of horses galloping, horns blowing and armour clinking together as armies prepare for battle!

This was one of Leonardo da Vinci's many detailed sketches of figures he would have seen in his daily life while wandering the cobbled streets of Milan and Florence.

Although he wasn't a soldier himself, Leonardo would have been no stranger to the art of war — a large part of his work for the regent of Milan was designing inventions for use in battle, and in 1502 da Vinci briefly became a military engineer for the infamous and ferocious warrior Cesare Borgia.

This drawing was completed using a technique called metalpoint. This involved first preparing a canvas by painting it with something called a 'ground', often made of chalk or bone ash. Then the artist would draw or carve into it using a metal tool, leaving tiny particles of metal on the 'ground' and creating their image.

Da Vinci probably used a fancy silver tool for his artwork, as this wouldn't become blunt as quickly as lead or tin tools and allowed him to draw very precise lines. Working this way meant Leonardo could create a portrait with a great deal of detail but it would have taken a very long time to finish!

Unfinished paintings

As far as we know, Leonardo completed less than 20 artworks over the course of his career. Of course, there are probably several other paintings and drawings that he completed but have been lost over the years or have never been seen by another person. For someone as prolific as da Vinci, under 20 artworks doesn't seem like a huge amount for a lifetime of work.

A major reason why we don't see more of da Vinci's work hanging in galleries around the world today is his tendency to leave paintings unfinished. Leonardo would often either lose interest in what he was doing, or get distracted by other projects, whether they were designing buildings, tinkering with his latest inventions or possibly his musical endeavours.

It's clear that even the most talented people have difficulties and struggles sometimes! Leonardo was very hard on himself and felt he was a failure for leaving things unfinished. Now we can look back on his work centuries later and see he was not a failure at all — he was one of the most talented artists we've ever seen!

Architecture

Leonardo da Vinci explored many different fields in his lifetime. One of these was architecture, the complicated practice of designing buildings. He was well-suited for this task as it brings together many of his areas of expertise including science, art and mathematics. Leonardo's artistic ability influenced his architectural designs greatly and allowed him to create highly detailed and technical drawings, something that is still important in architecture today. Although none of his designs were ever built, his brilliant mind and sketches didn't go to waste. Da Vinci has had a great influence on architecture as we know it today, and the beautiful buildings he designed are still looked at and studied with great interest.

Etruscan Mausoleum

Architecture is a crucial first step when designing a new building. It's important to know how the building will be engineered and if it will be structurally safe. Da Vinci's keen eye for art also helped him to design elegant and elaborate structures, from intimidating castles to domed cathedrals, tall towers to soaring spires!

One of his stranger architectural plans was the Etruscan Mausoleum. This structure consisted of six different compartments, and was inspired by Etruscan architecture which came from centuries before da Vinci. The Etruscan civilisation was part of Ancient Rome and was well-known for skills in architecture and building.

France

Rome to France

In 1516 at the age of 64, Leonardo moved from Rome (where he had been working since 1513) to Amboise in France, where he spent the remainder of his life. Da Vinci received the invitation to move by the French King Francis I who wanted Leonardo to become his resident artist and inventor. It is possible that he had the help of a trusty mule to get all the way to France, but mule or no mule this would have been a giant trip through rolling hills and the freezing Alps. Leonardo must have been exhausted by the end of such a long journey and ready to enjoy the manor house awaiting him in Amboise.

Milan

Da Vinci's life and legacy

Leonardo da Vinci spent the last few years of his life in Amboise and continued to paint, study and invent right up until his death in 1519. Over the course of his lifetime he achieved a truly remarkable amount. Da Vinci created some of the world's most famous paintings, dreamt up amazing inventions, pushed forward human understanding of anatomy and the natural world, and so much more! Even with these countless achievements though, Leonardo was very hard on himself and often felt like a failure because of his unfinished or unsuccessful projects. So if you ever feel down on yourself, just remember even a genius like the great Leonardo da Vinci didn't get it right every time!

Da Vinci's passion for sketching and note-taking has given us an amazing insight into the life and mind of this fascinating Renaissance polymath. It's believed that he produced over 50 notebooks during his lifetime, all bursting with wild ideas, futuristic inventions, fearsome creatures and beautiful works of art. Some of these books have sadly been lost or destroyed over the centuries, but many can be found in art galleries or private collections around the globe. Who knows what hidden wonders may have been buried deep within da Vinci's lost notebooks!

The value of da Vinci's work

When we look at Leonardo's work today, it is some of the most highly valued artwork in all of history. You won't believe the massive sums that his works have sold for . . .

1. The 'Codex Leicester'

One of Leonardo da Vinci's journals, this contains several of his scientific discoveries including findings around astronomy, fossils and the movement of water. It was bought by Bill Gates (the founder of Microsoft) for a massive 30.8 million US dollars!

2. The Salvator Mundi

This is a famous painting that was thought to be lost up until its discovery in 2005. After being restored and verified as authentic, the painting was sold at auction in 2017 for an astounding 450.3 million US dollars!

3. The Vitruvian Man

One of Leonardo's most famous and well-known drawings, this is currently in the Gallerie dell'Accademia in Venice, Italy. It's not technically for sale — but it is insured for at least 1 billion euros!

4. The Mona Lisa

Da Vinci's most famous and prized artwork currently hangs in the Louvre in Paris. Due to the fame and history of this iconic portrait, the painting isn't currently for sale, but the many visitors each year bring a huge amount of money to the French economy.

Da Vinci today

Even 500 years after his death we can see Leonardo da Vinci's influence all around us. Many of his inventions that may have seemed wacky are commonplace in today's world, thanks to his ability to think far beyond his time.

Although modern parachutes use much more sophisticated materials and techniques, the design is not overly different from what da Vinci dreamt up over 500 years ago. Both designs feature a large fabric cone (or an arch in today's parachutes) to create air resistance. This air resistance slows down the skydiver as they descend, allowing them to land safely.

It's possible that without da Vinci's fascination for human flight we may not have planes, helicopters, or air travel as we know it. Although Leonardo never lived to see humans fly, I'm sure he would have been amazed at the giant bird-like passenger planes we have gliding through the skies today!

Some of the first functional diving suits closely resembled da Vinci's design, even using tubes connecting the diving suit to an oxygen source on the surface. Since then, modern diving suits have developed this design by allowing divers to take oxygen tanks underwater with them, freeing them up to swim through the water instead of simply walking along the ocean floor. However these suits unfortunately don't include Leonardo's bathroom bottle solution.

Da Vinci's legacy and inspiration lives on even in some of the most advanced technologies of the modern day. The 'da Vinci Surgical System' is a high-tech robot that can perform intricate operations in a much less invasive manner than humans can. The machine's name honours the great polymath for his detailed study of human anatomy and invention of the first ever robot!

"The noblest pleasure is the joy of understanding"
— Leonardo da Vinci